St Patrick Day
Mazes Book

This Book Belongs To:

_____

_____

St Patrick's Day Mazes Book
FOR KIDS AGES 8-12

Copyright © 2024 by
All rights reserved. No part of this book may be reproduced or used
in any form or by any means electronic or mechanical, including
scanning or recording, without the express written permission of the
author except for the use of brief quotations in a book review.

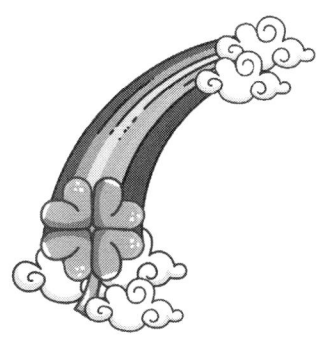

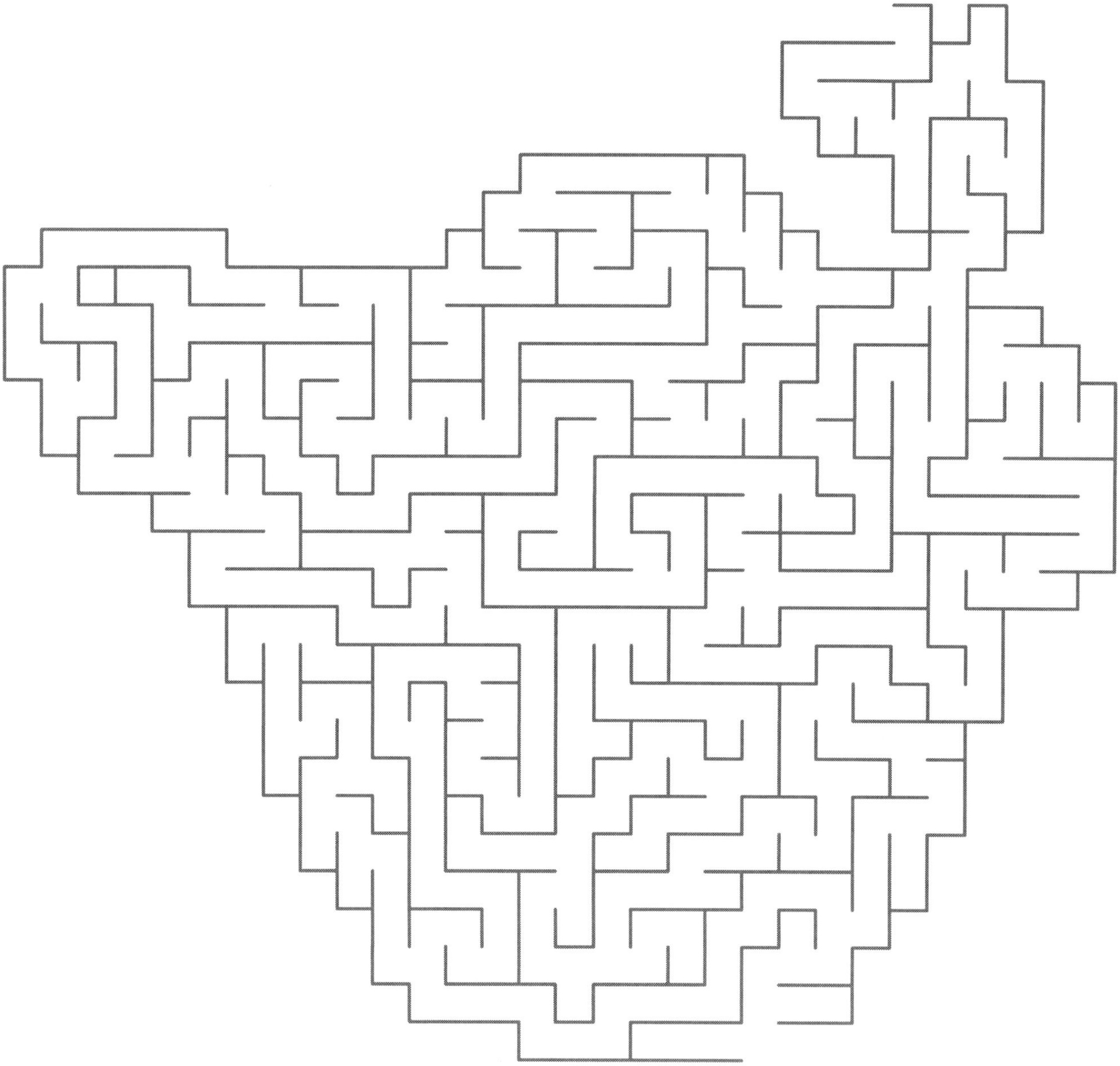

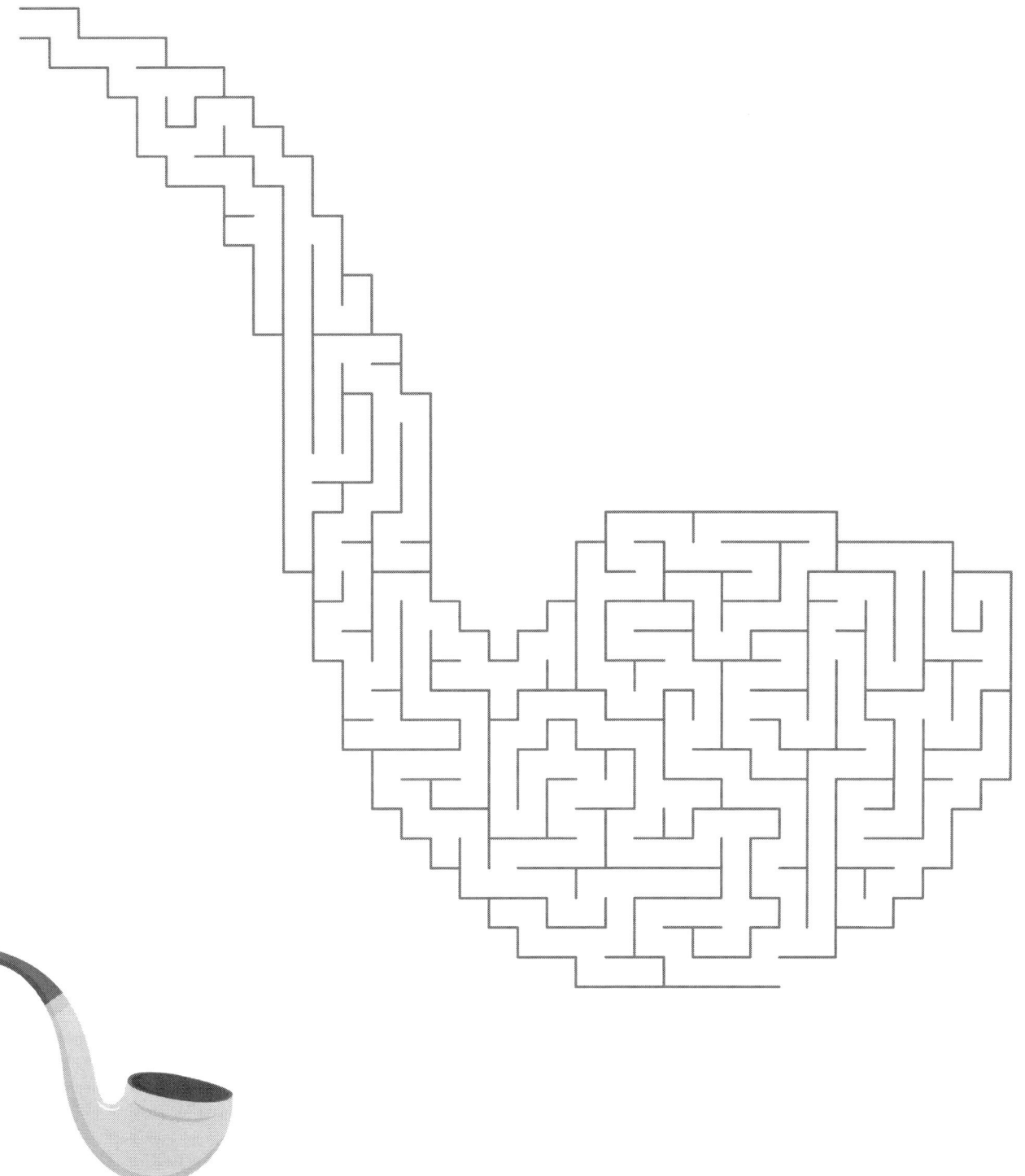

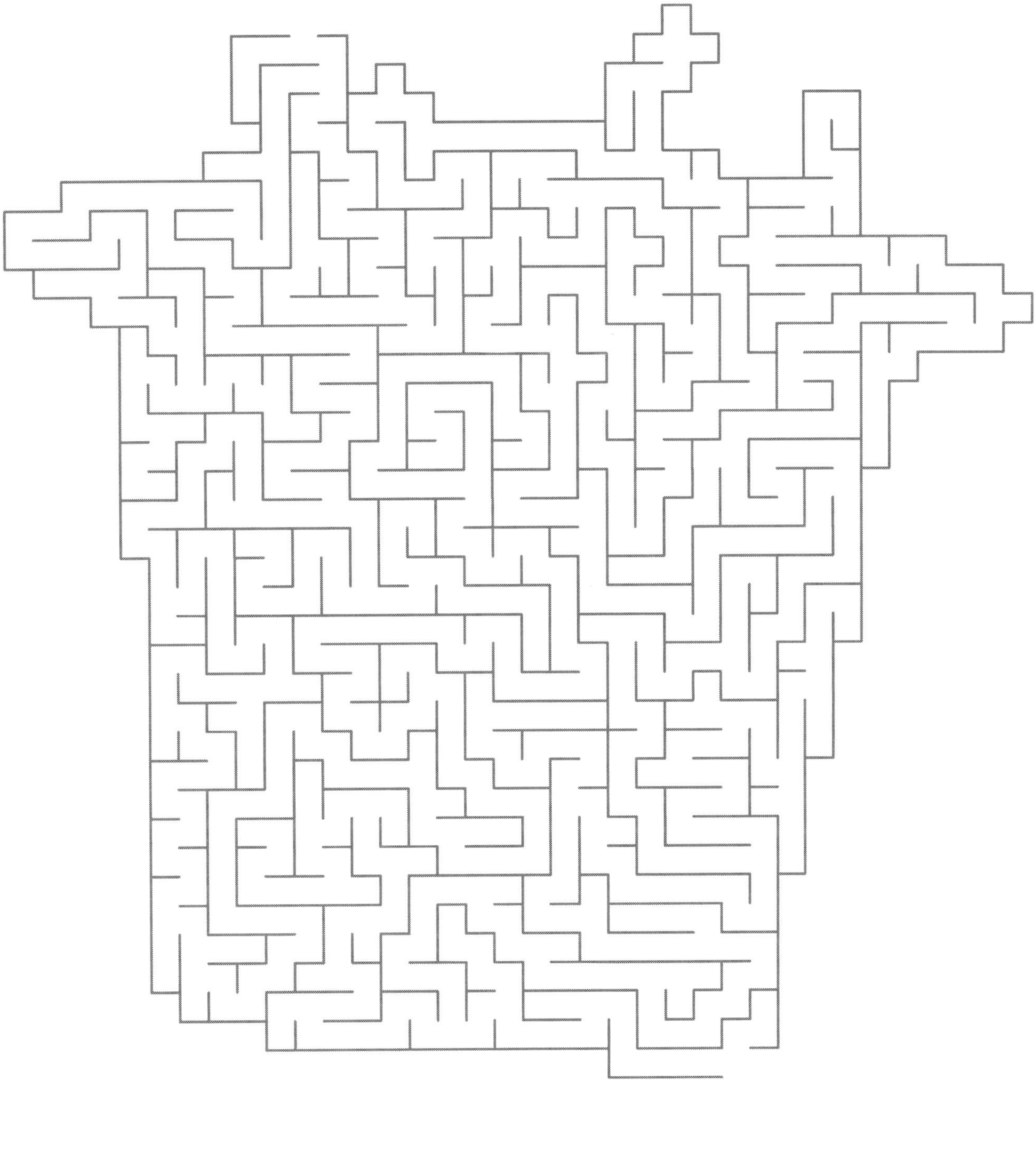

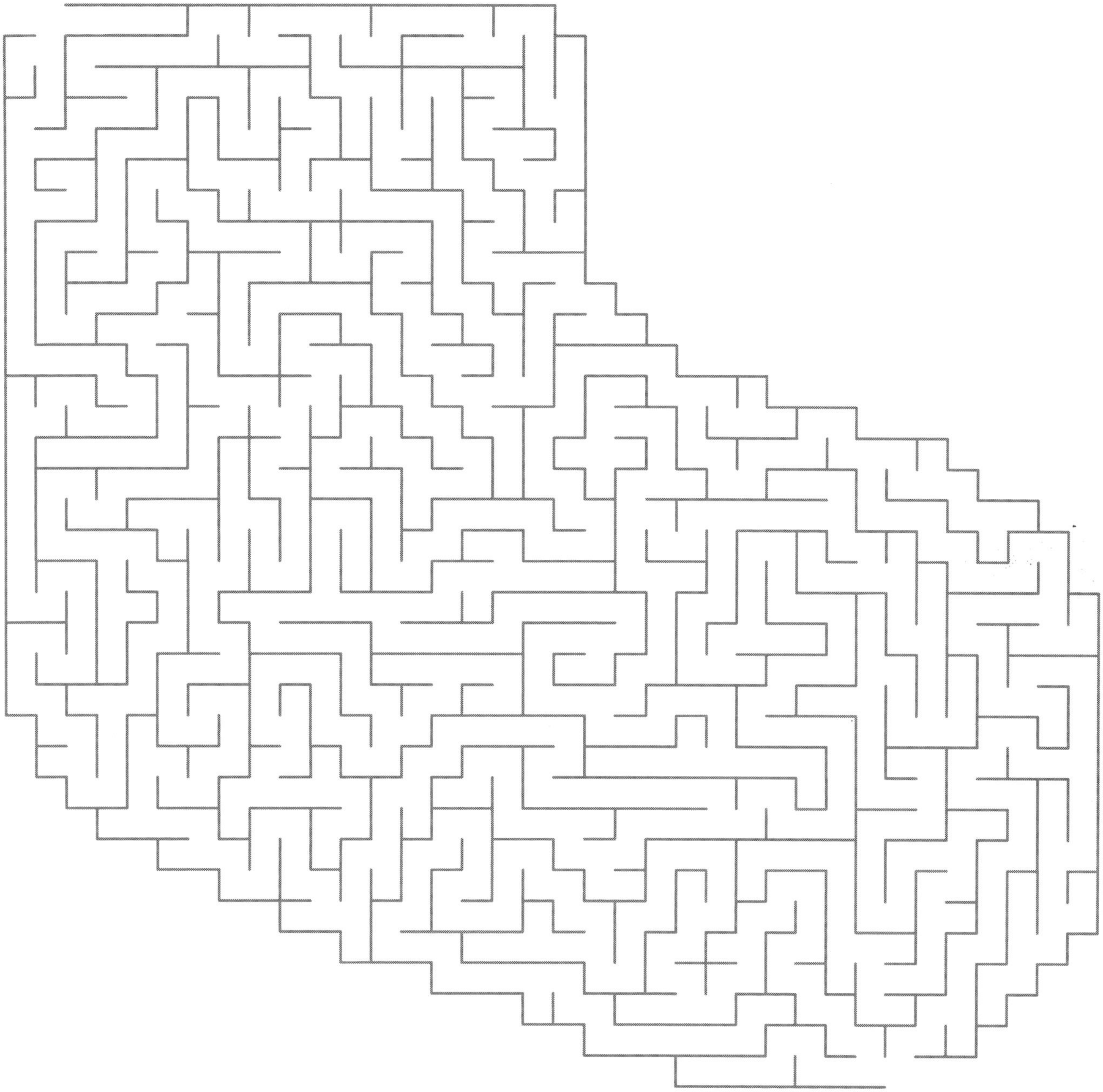

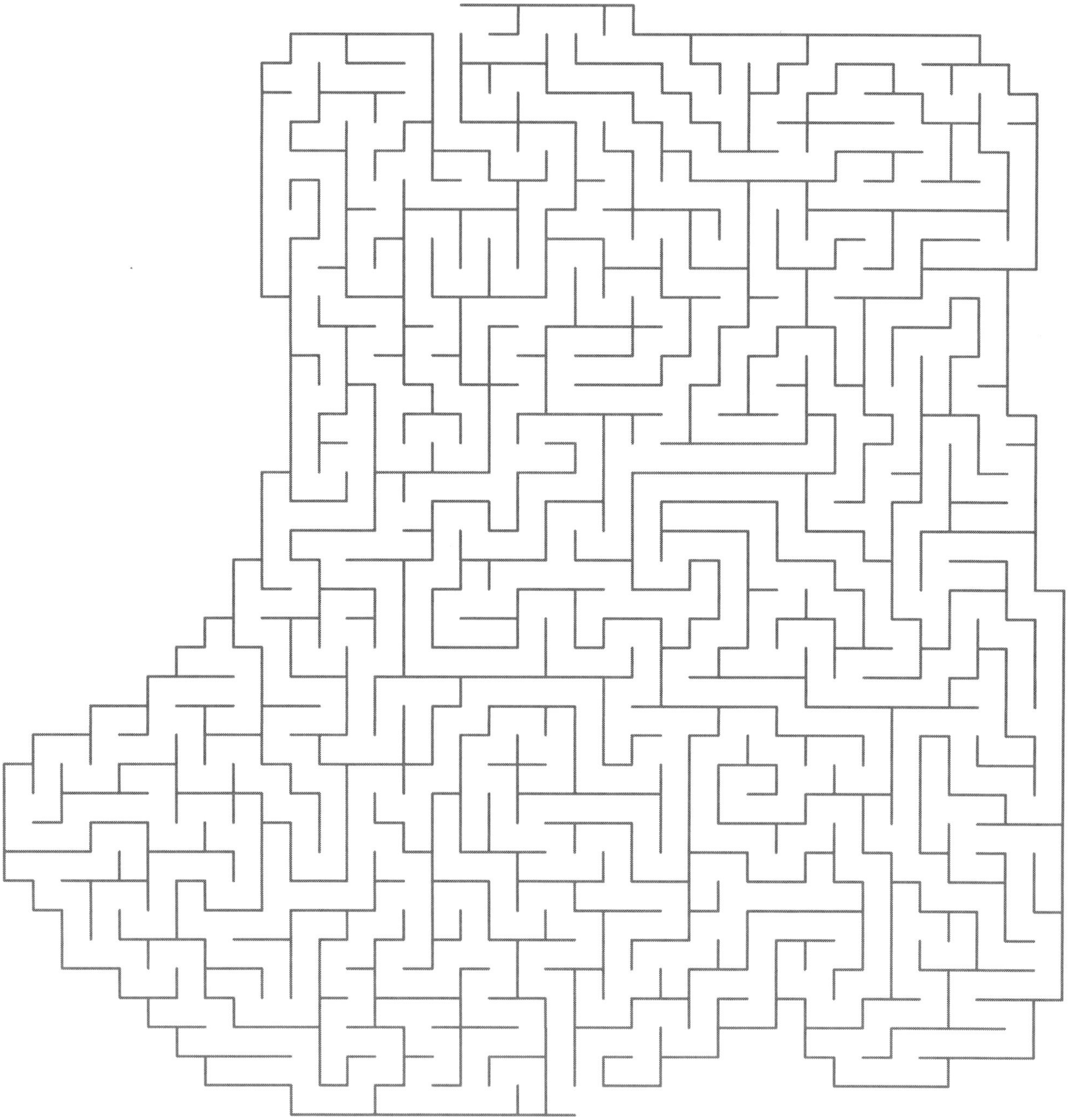

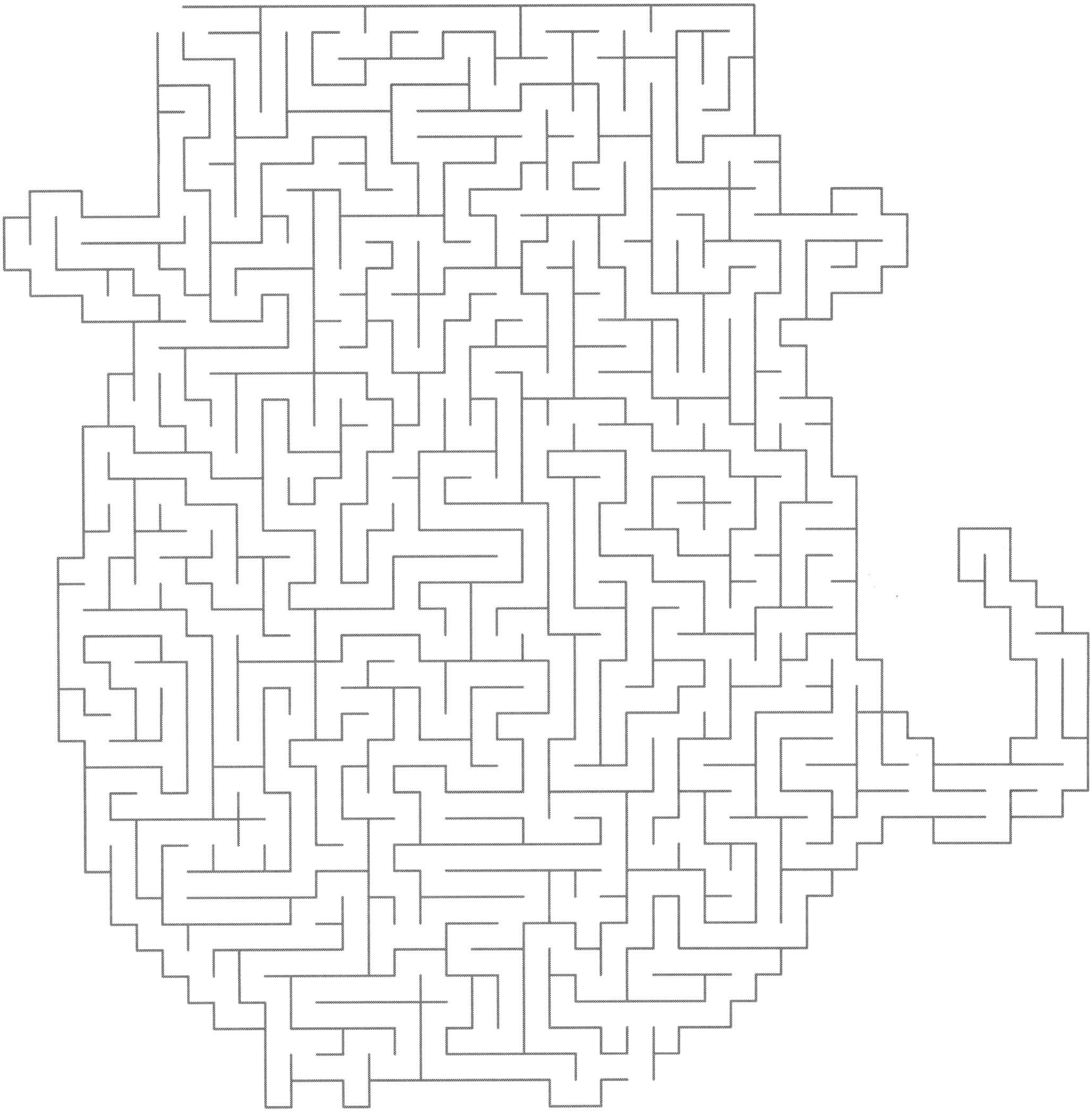

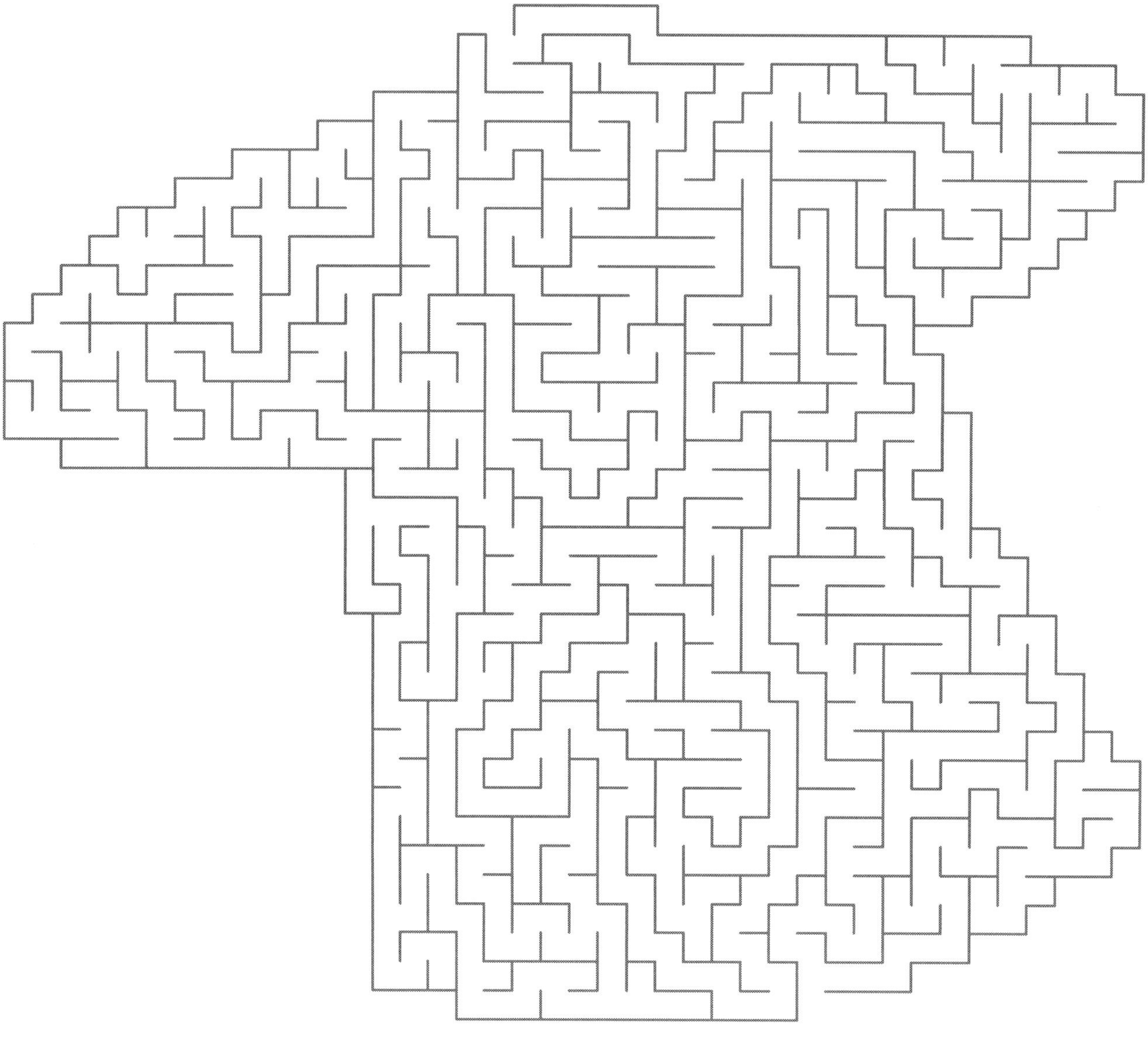

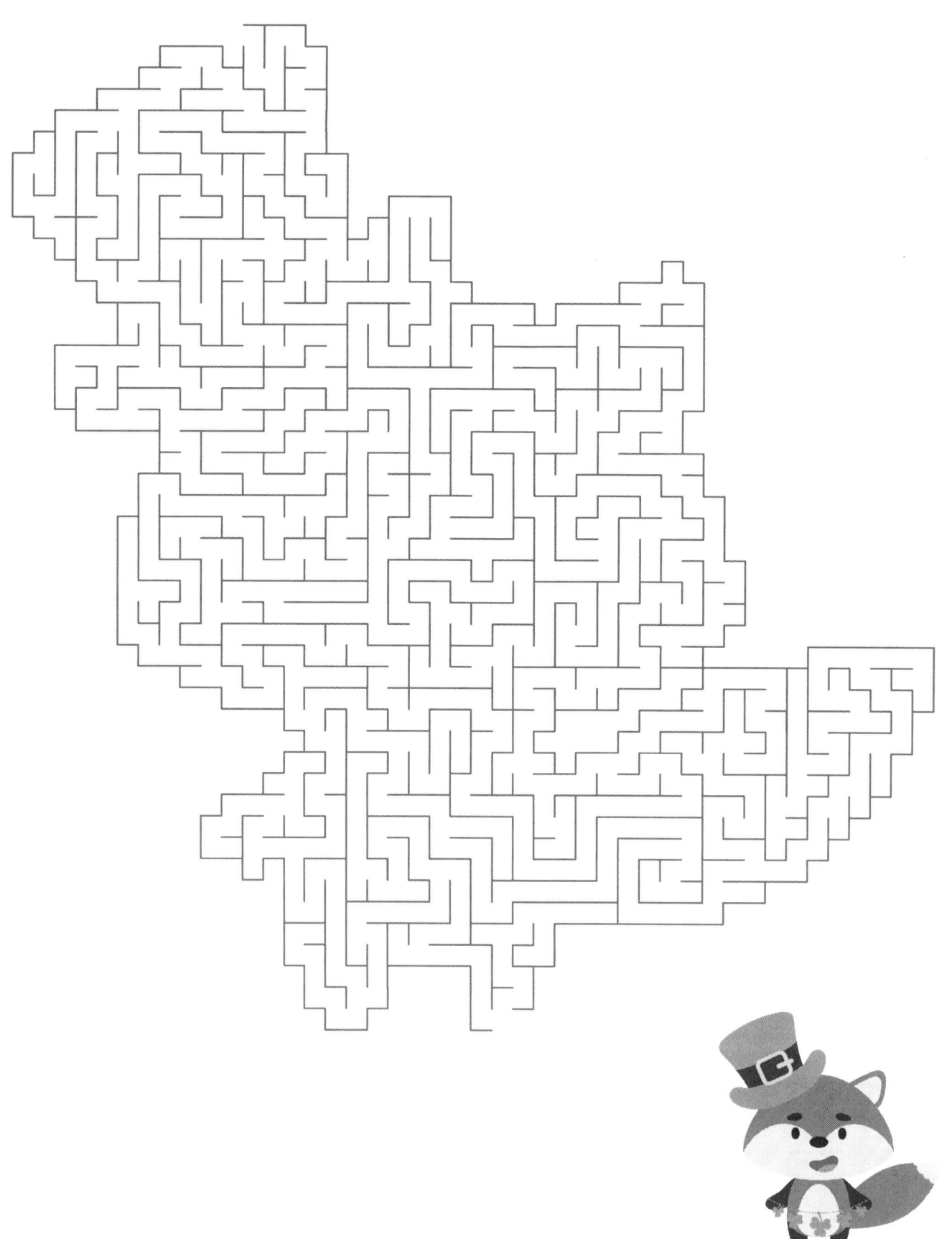

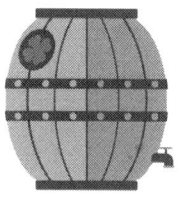

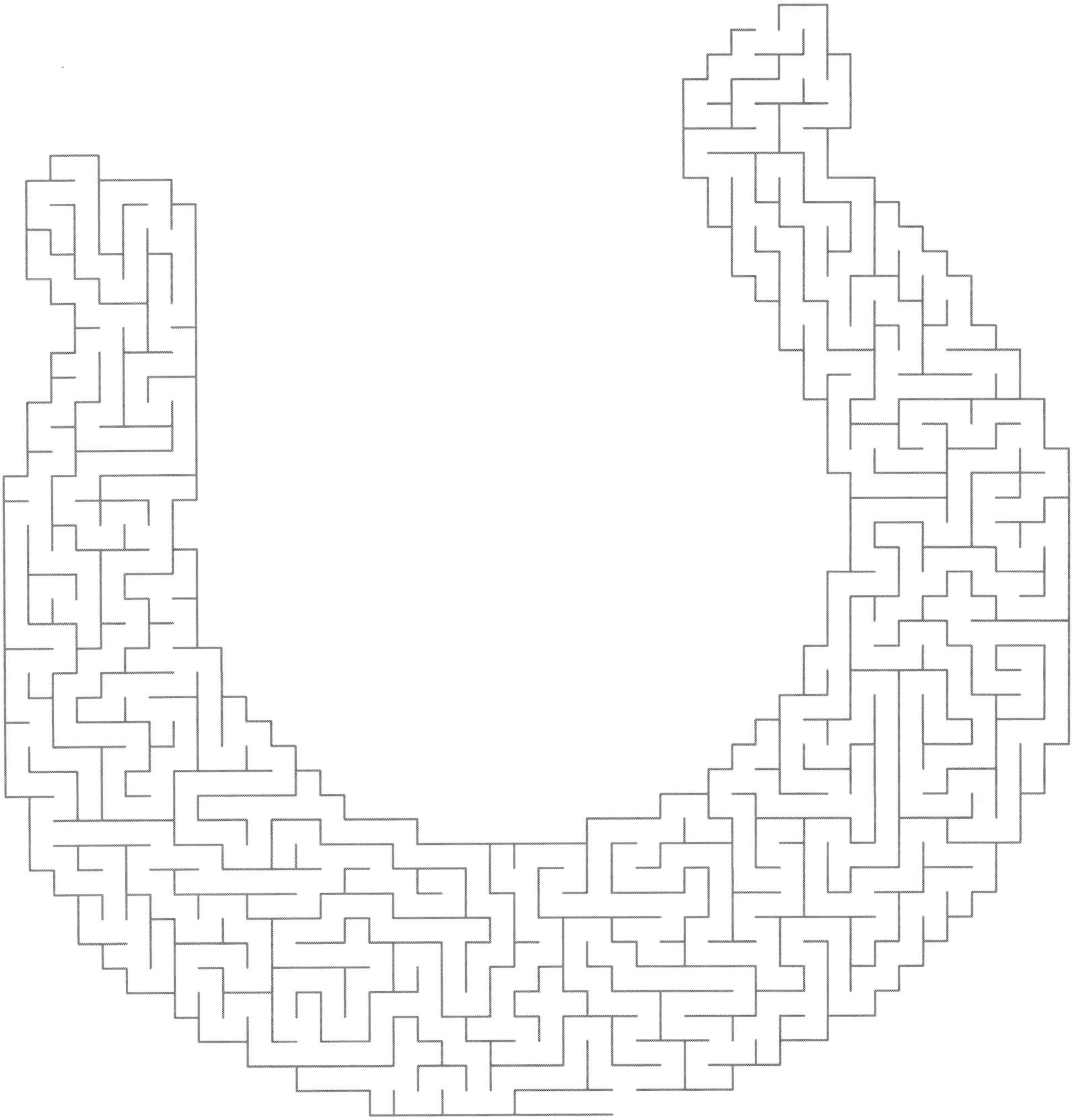

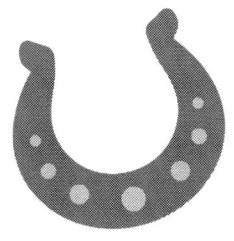

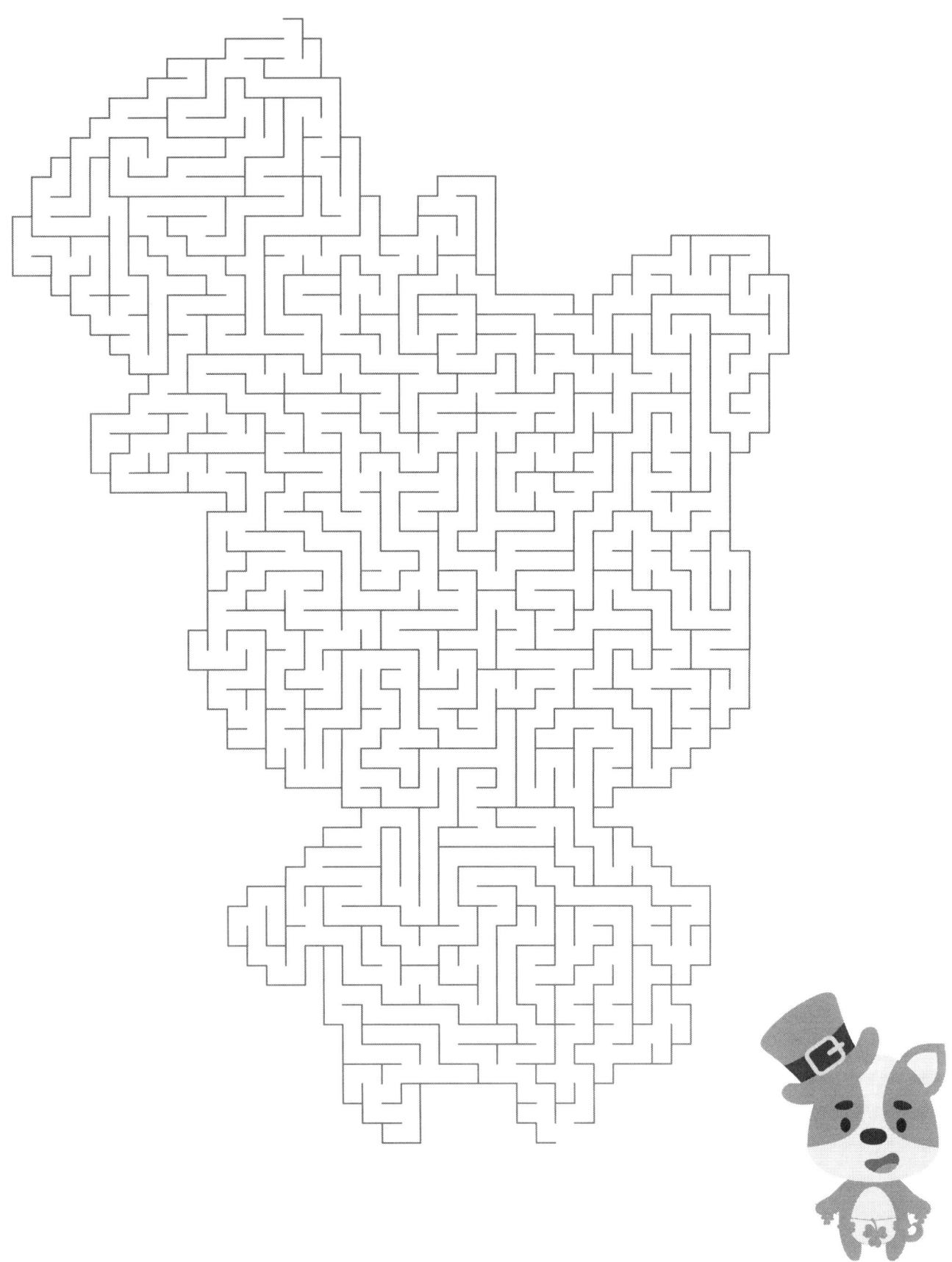

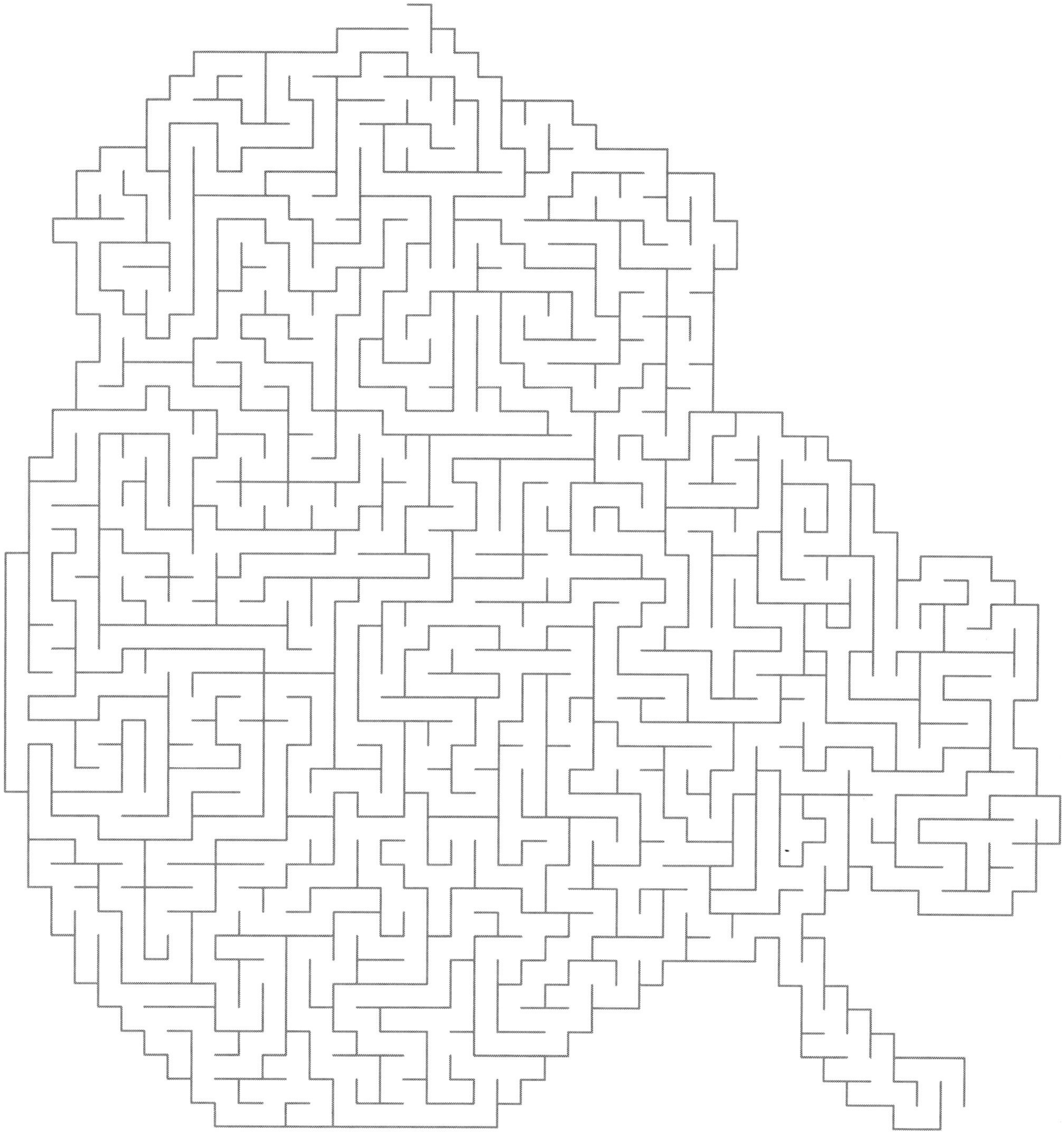

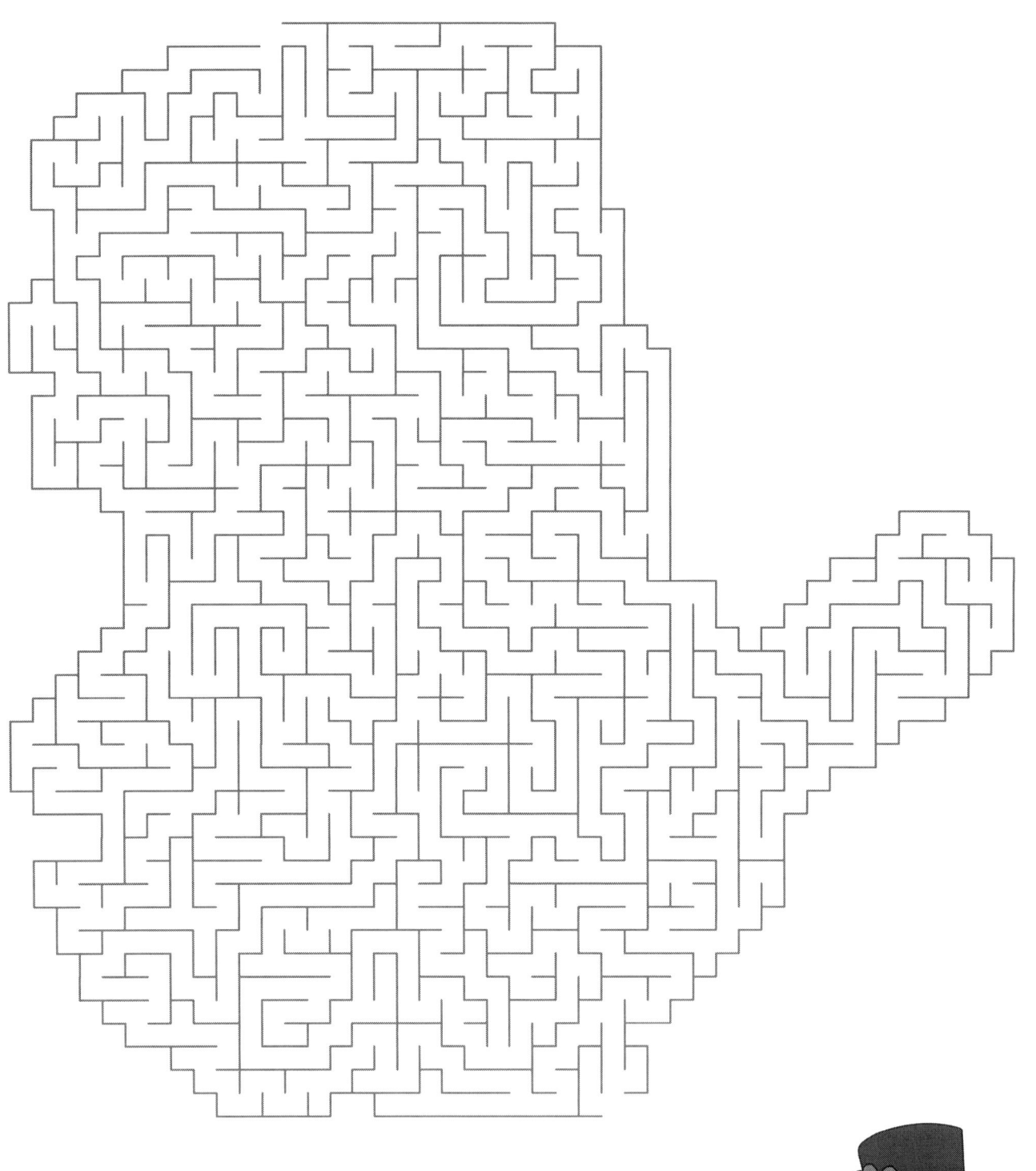

Page 42

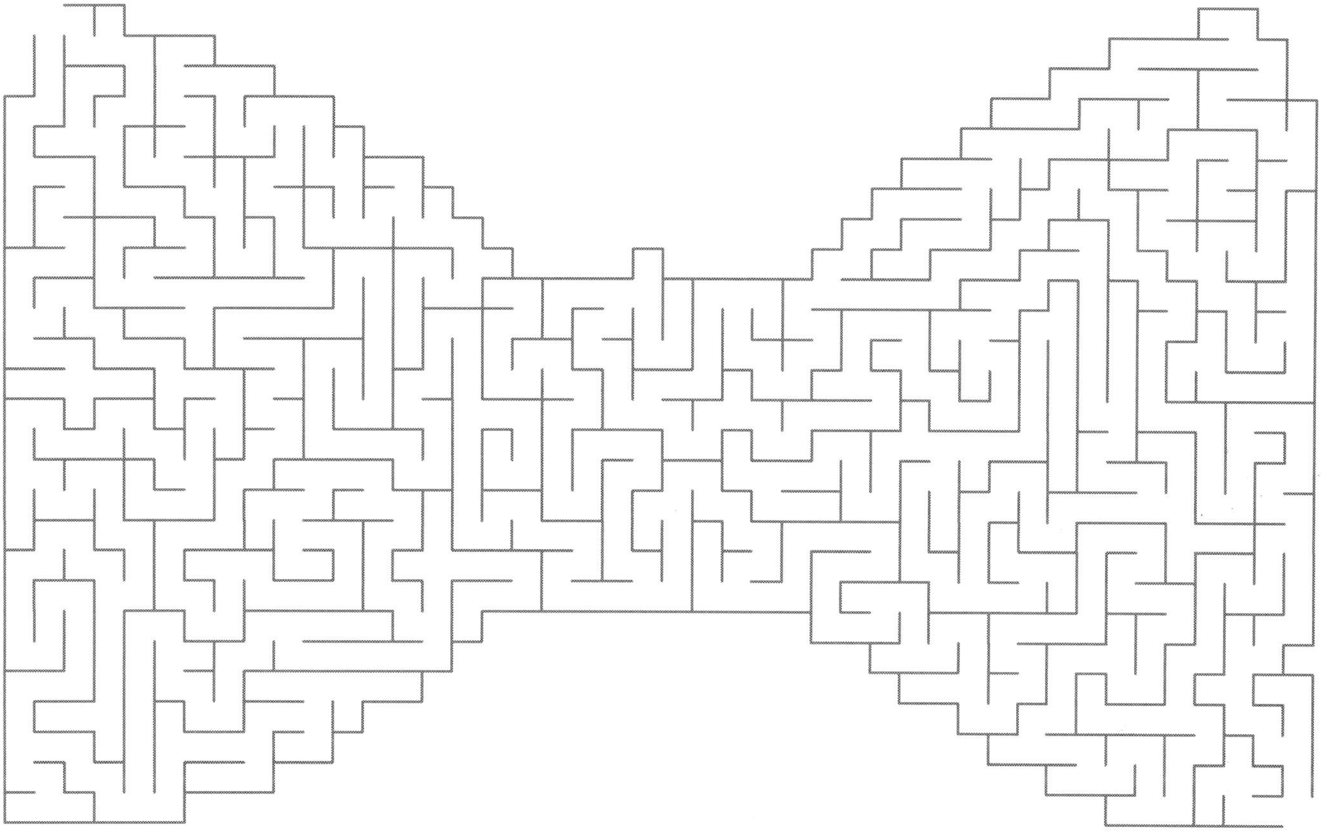

Solutions

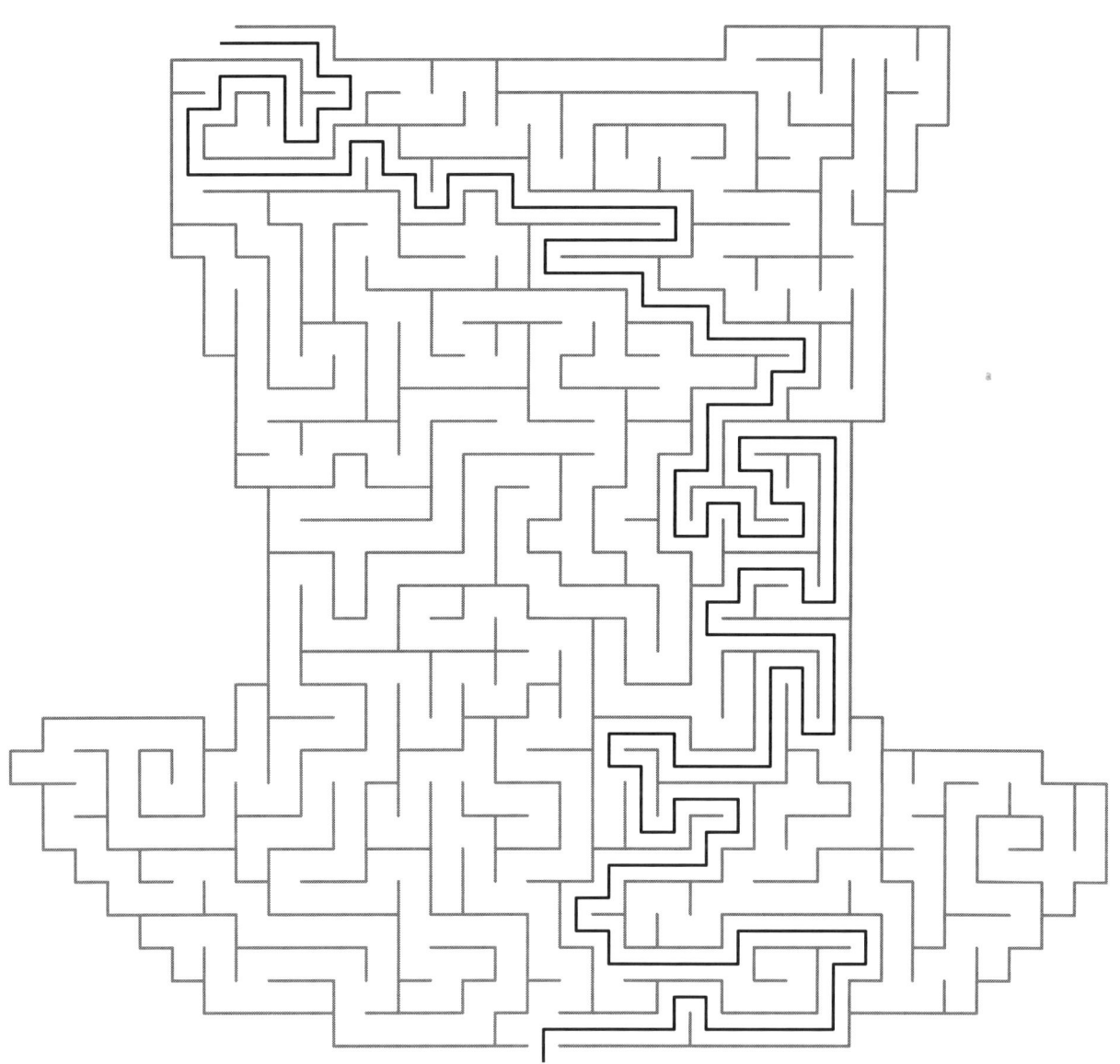

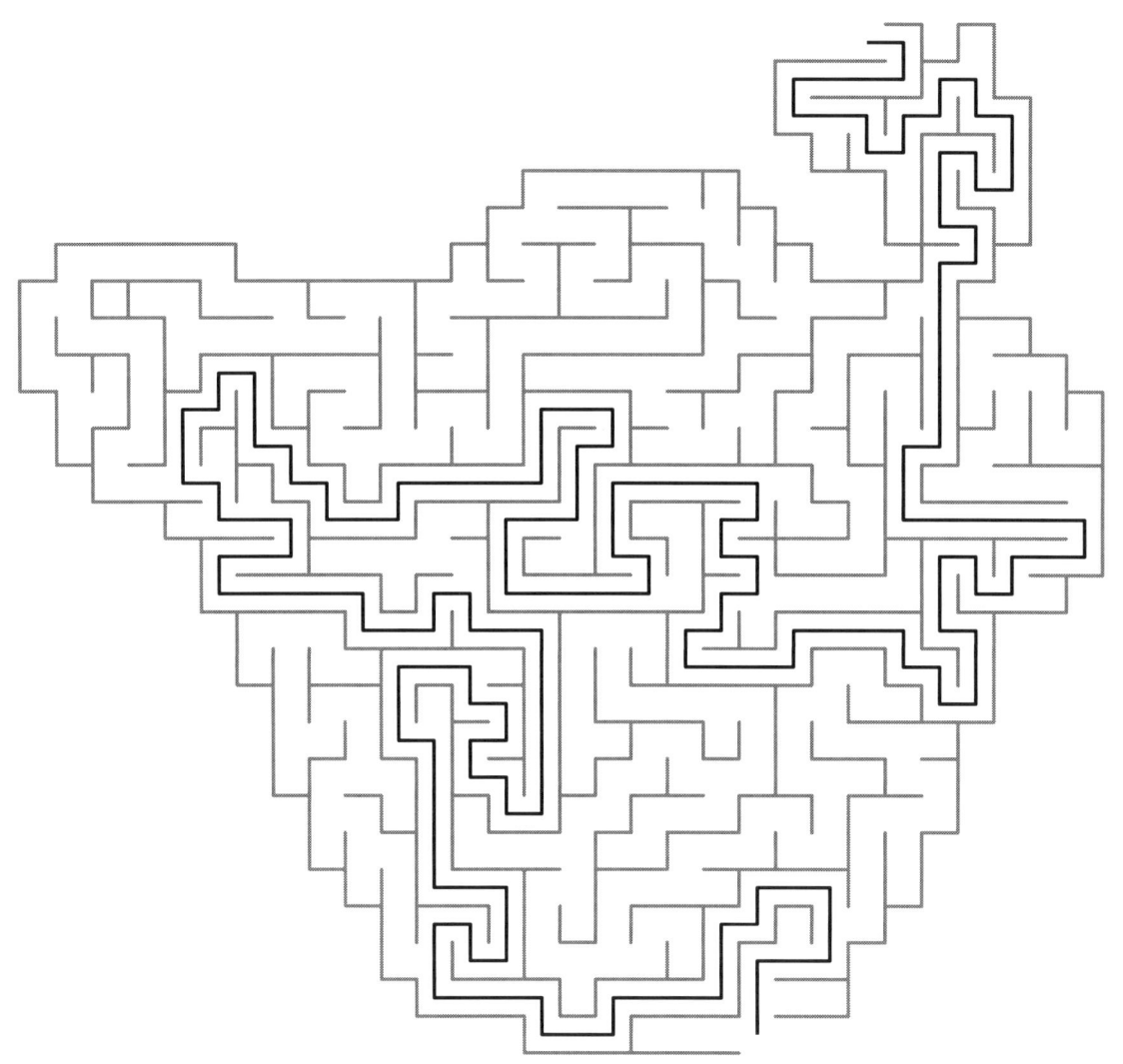

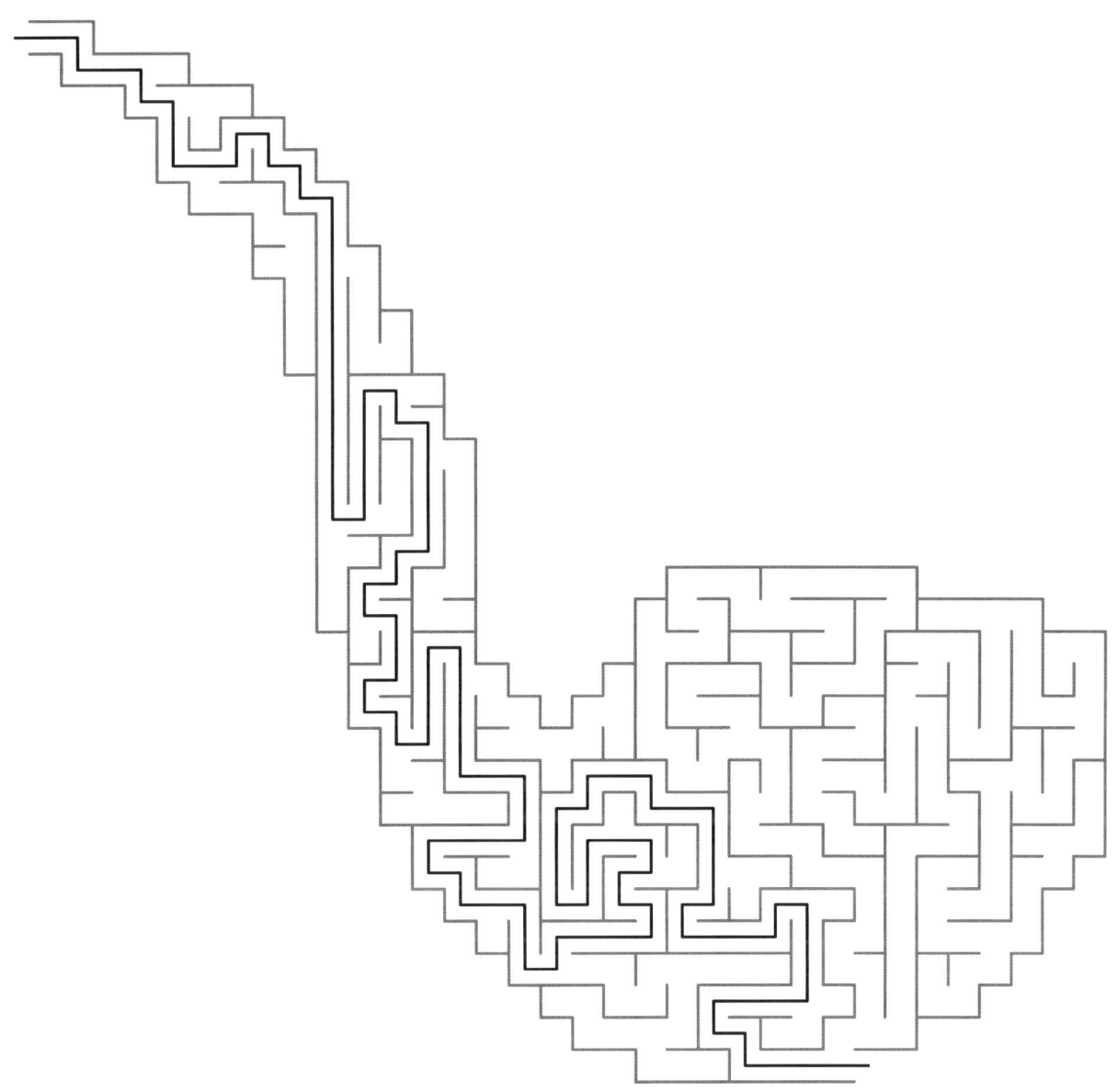

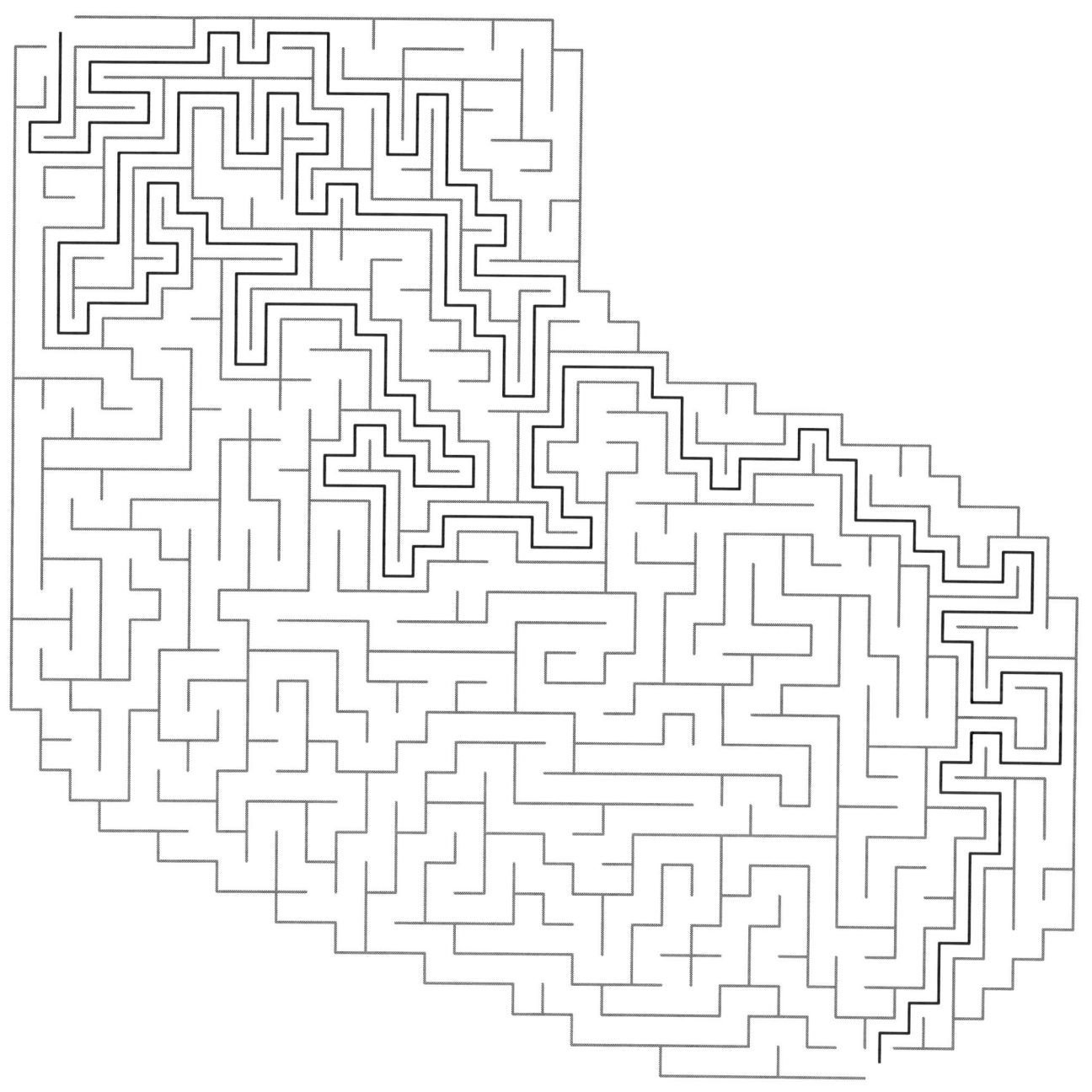

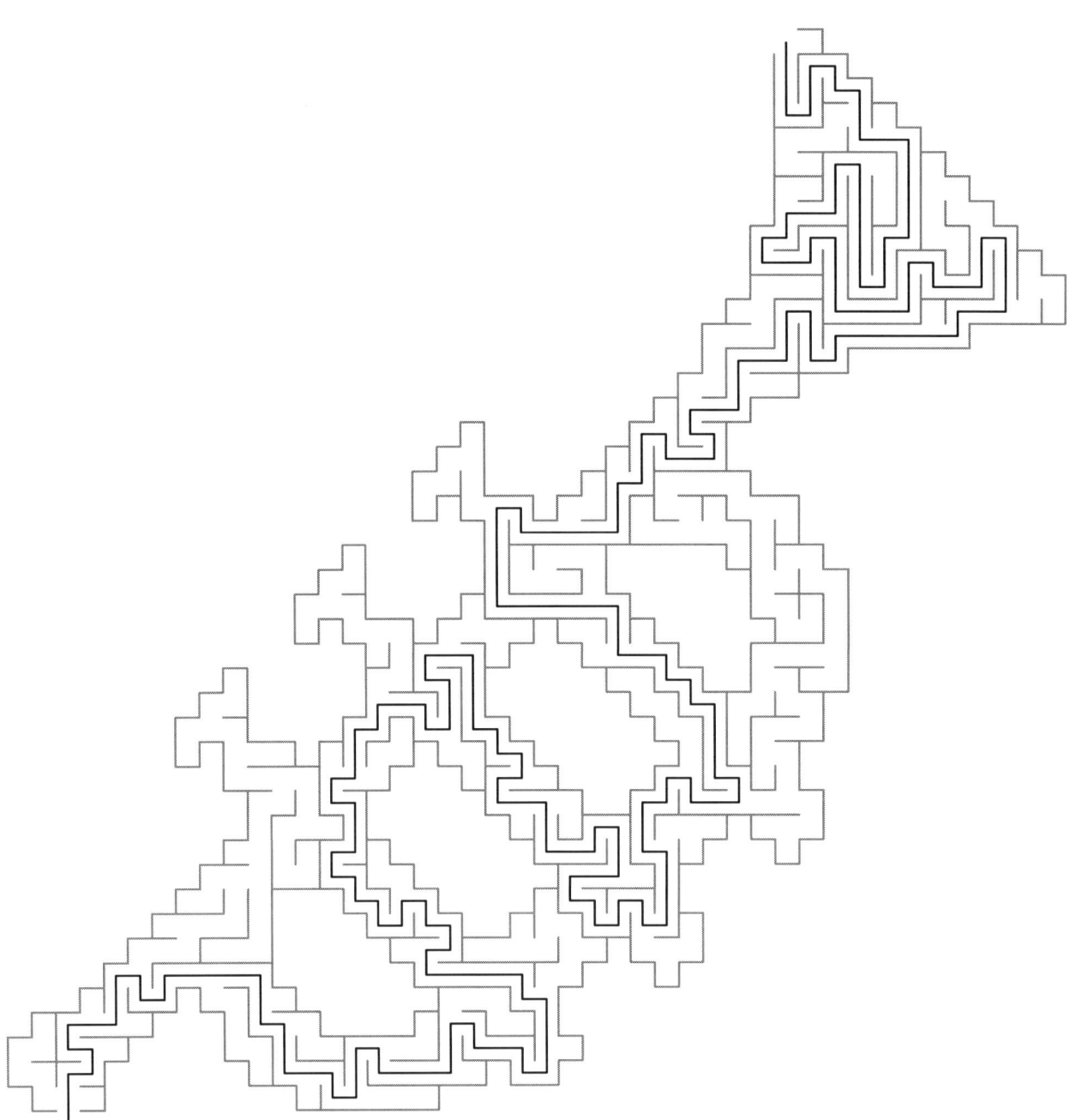

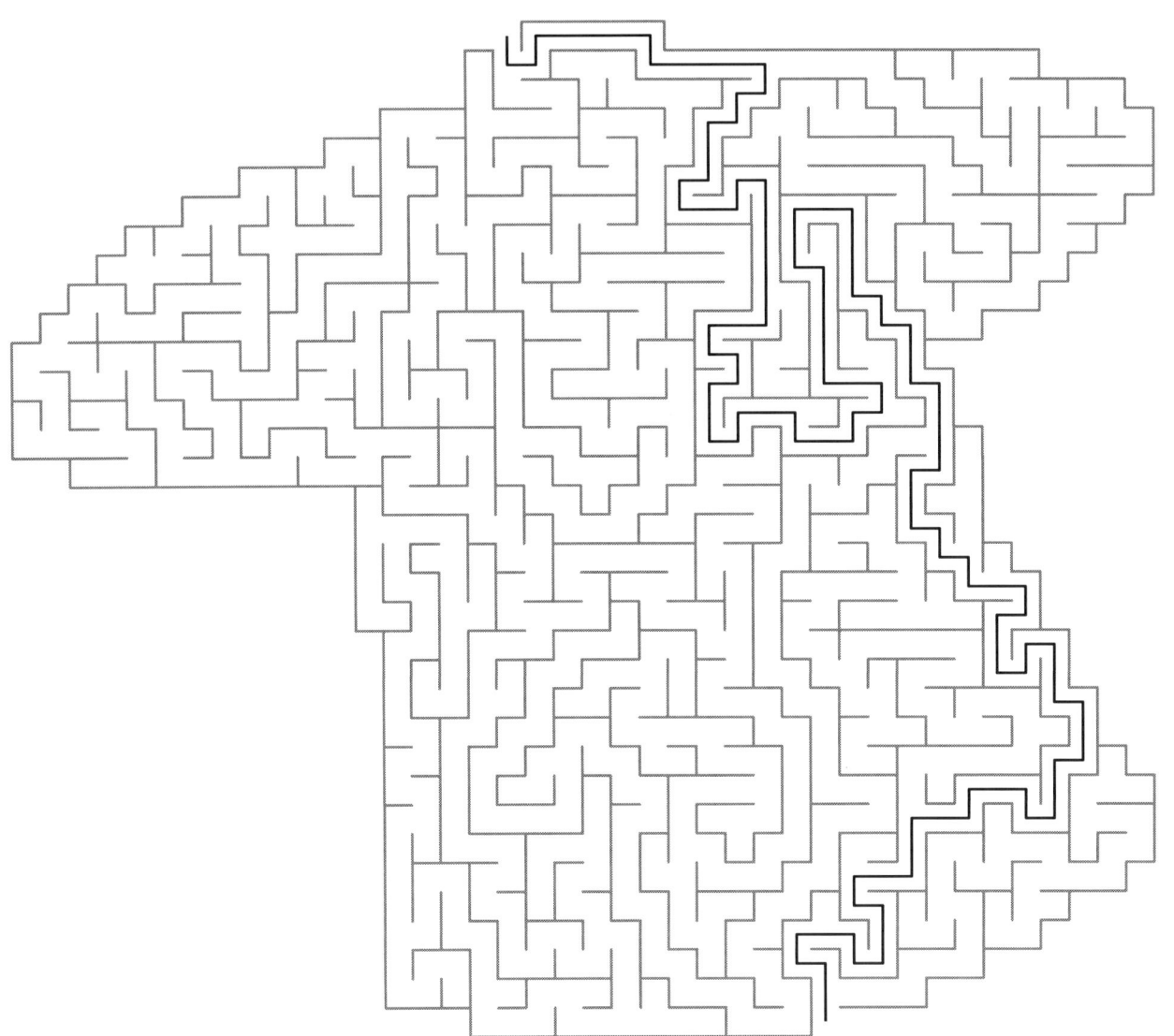

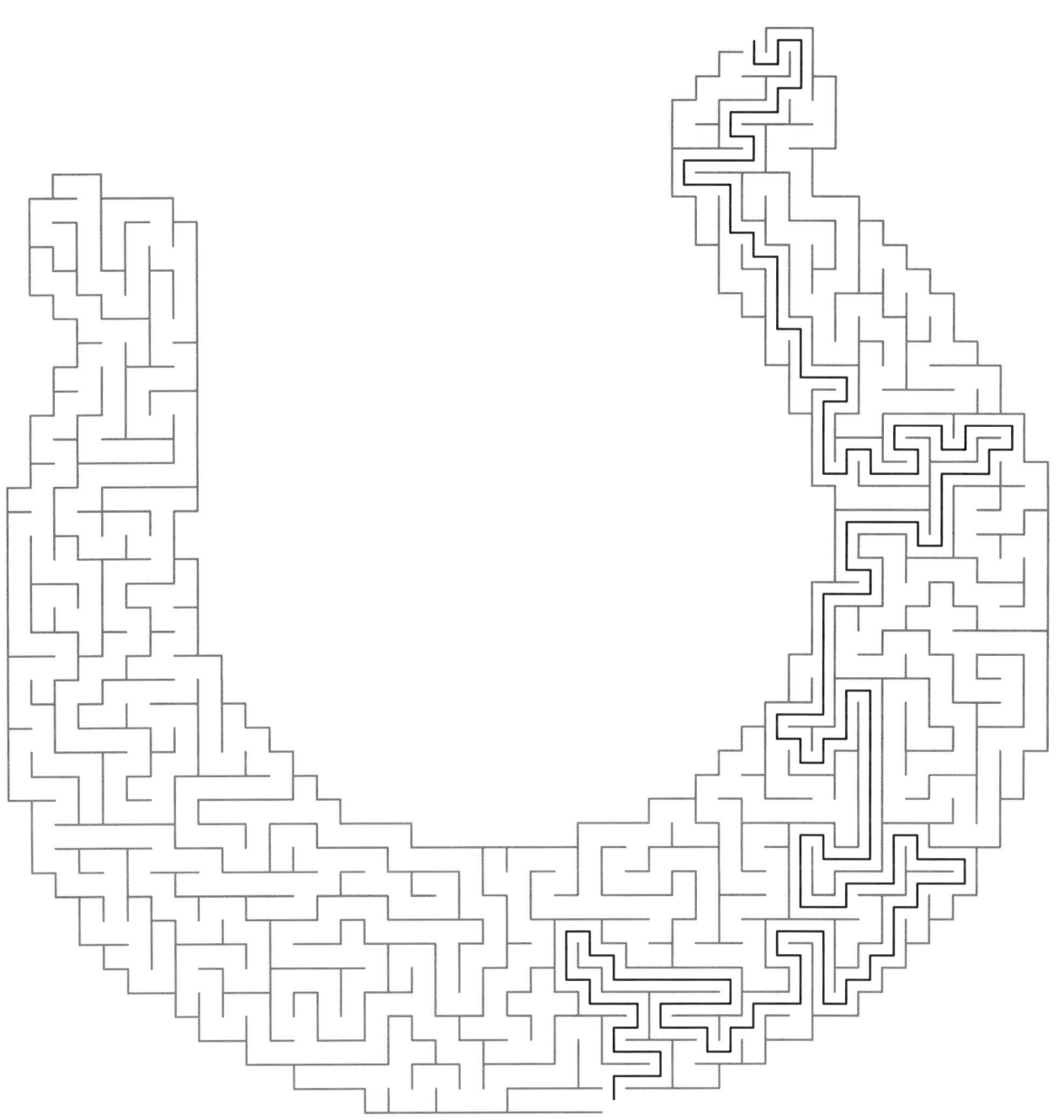

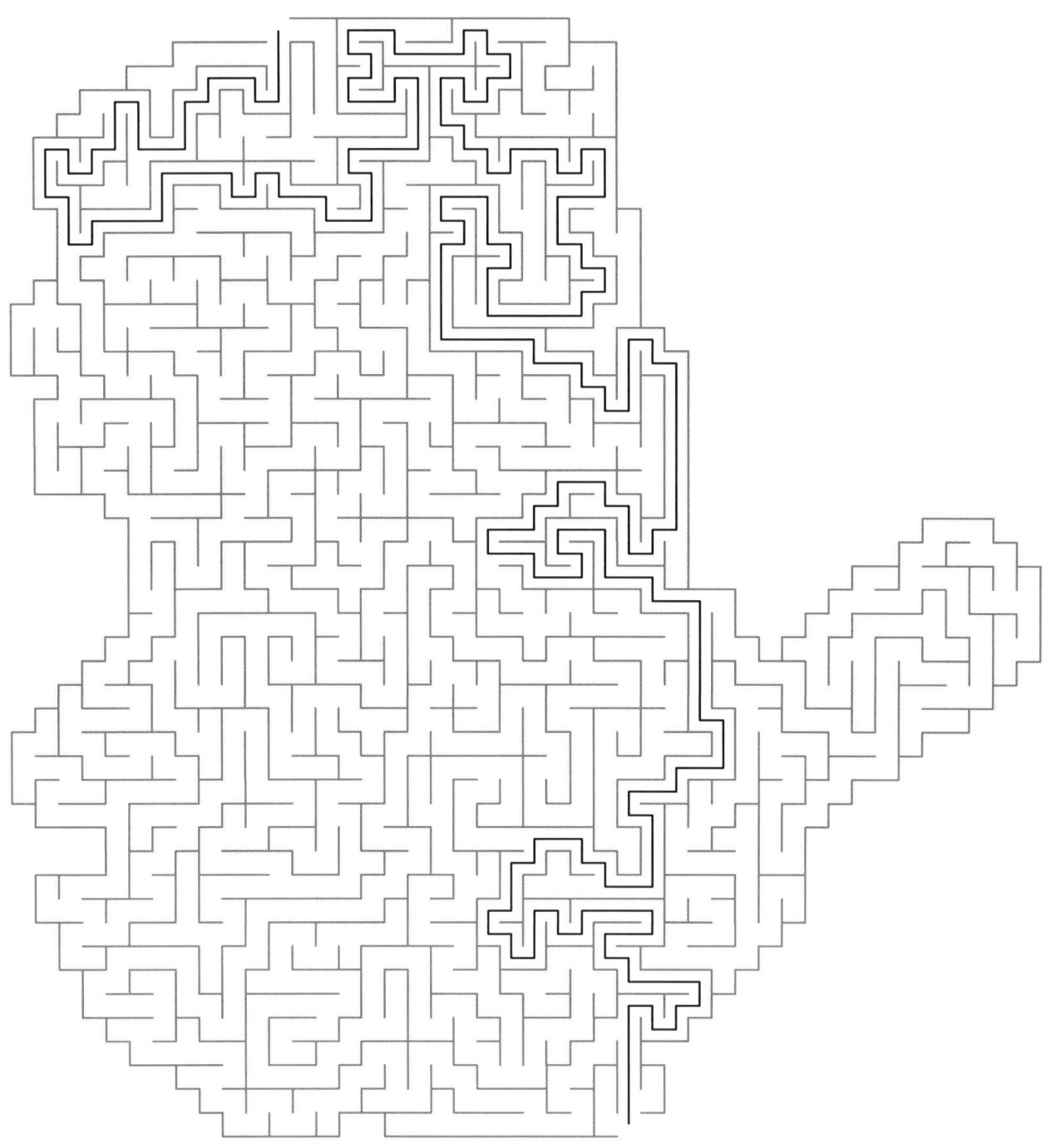

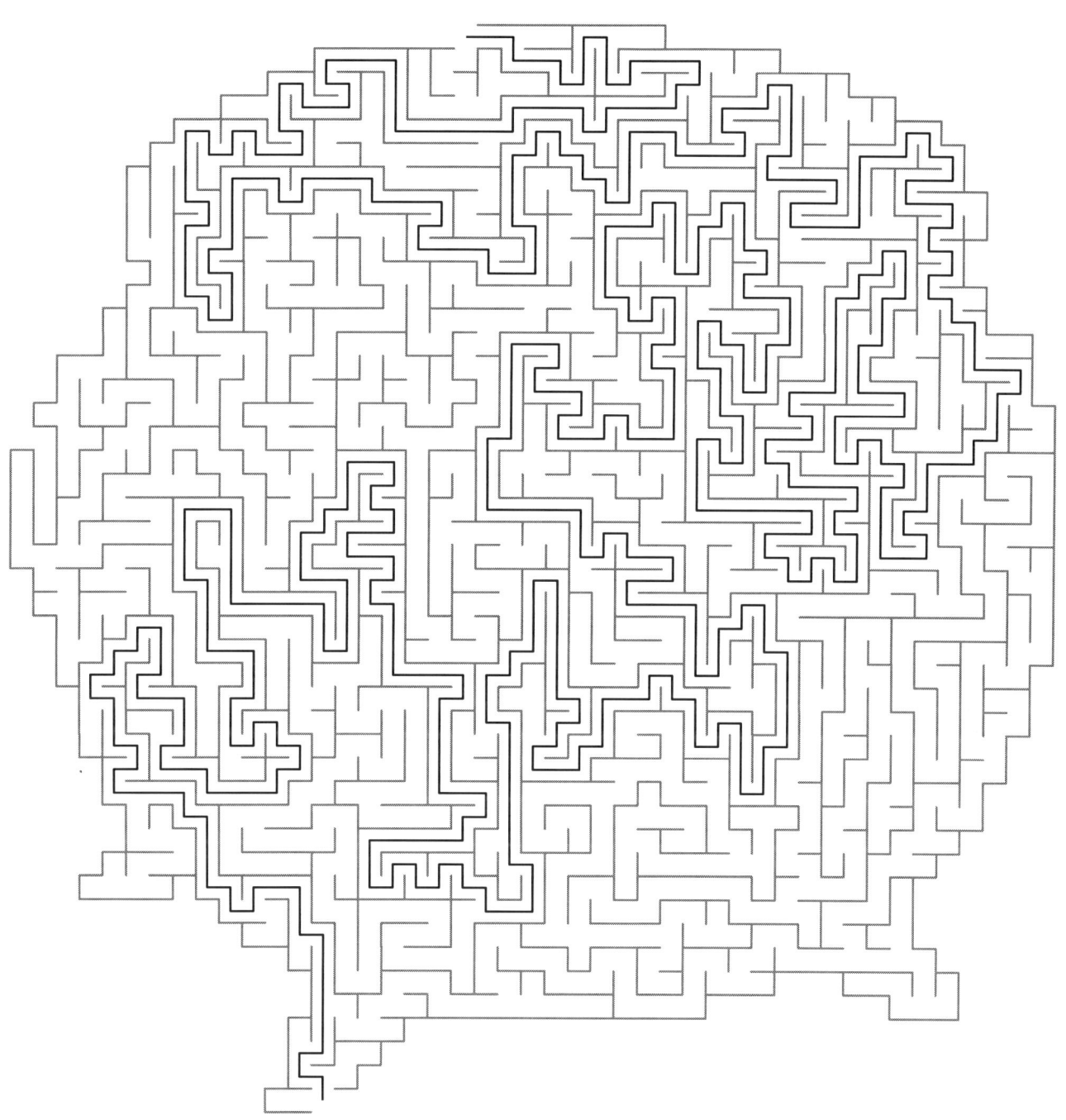

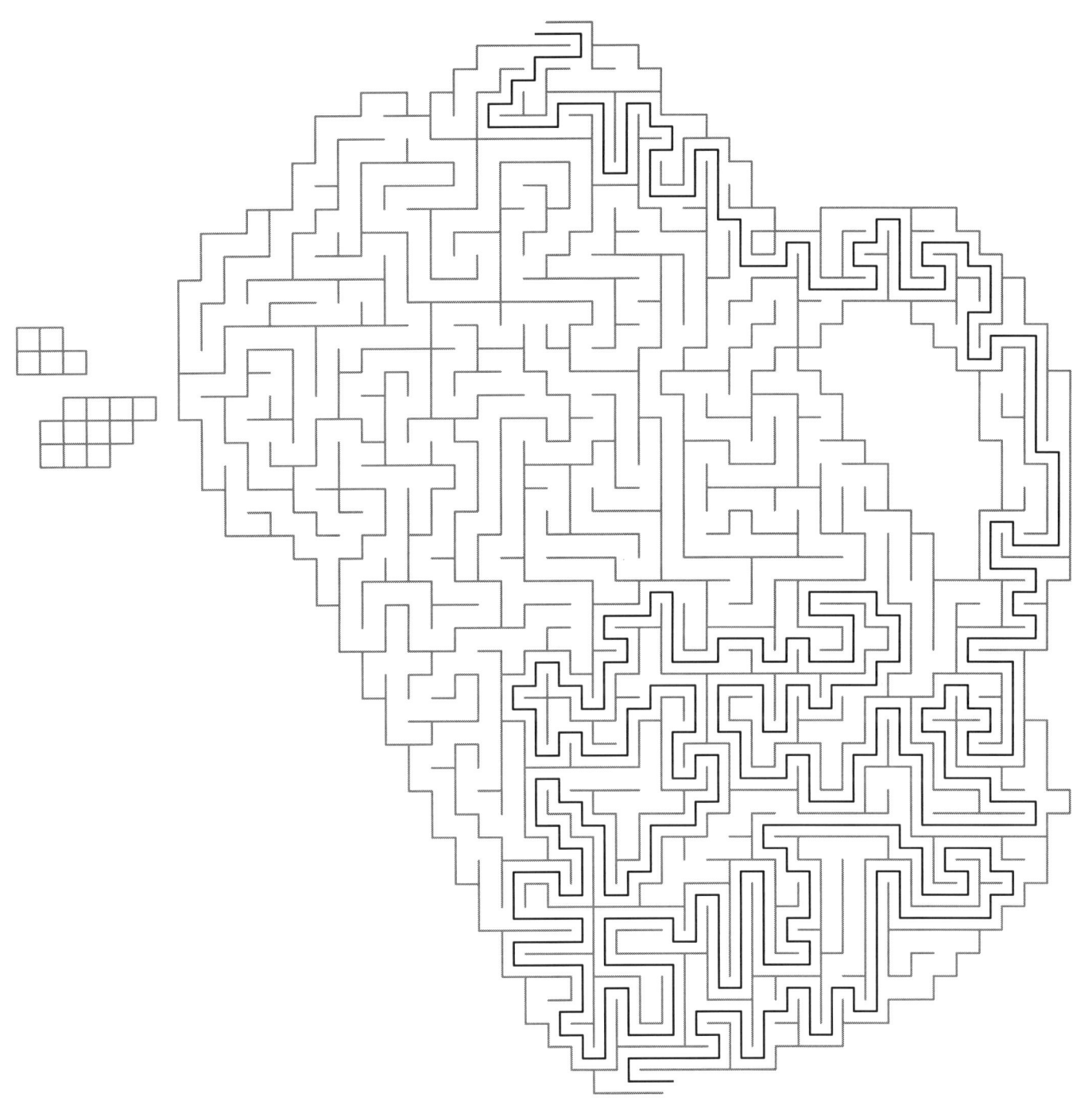

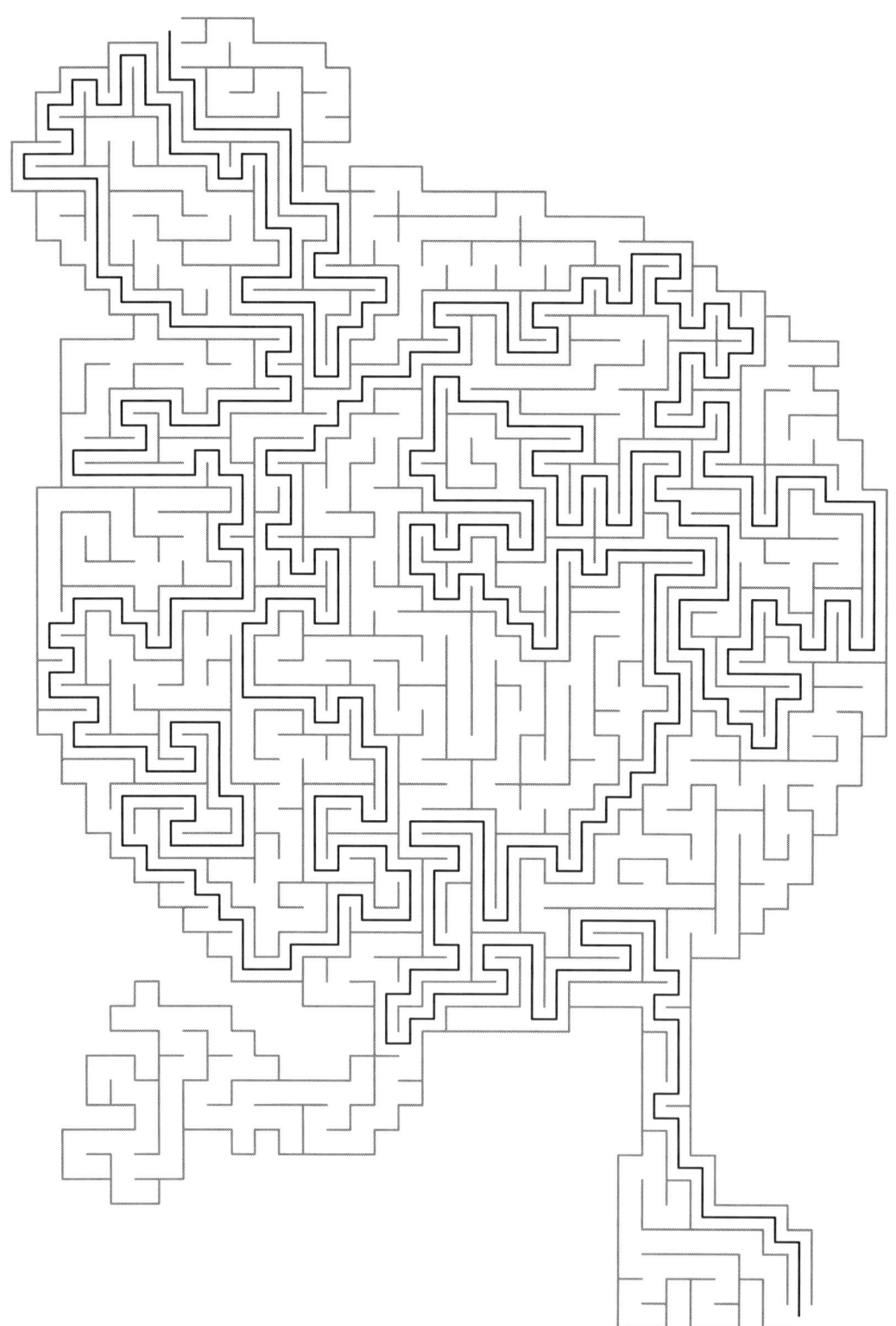